C000096943

Wiltshire: Life & Times

IN ASSOCIATION WITH THE WILTSHIRE TIMES

Wiltshire: Life & Times

IN ASSOCIATION WITH THE WILTSHIRE TIMES

Wiltshire Times

breedon **books**
PUBLISHING

First published in Great Britain in 2004 by
The Breedon Books Publishing Company Limited
Breedon House, 3 The Parker Centre,
Derby, DE21 4SZ.

ISBN 1 85983 427 2

Printed and bound by Butler & Tanner, Frome, Somerset.

Contents

Acknowledgements

Wiltshire: Life & Times compiled by Glenn Phillips, Trevor Porter and Holly Robinson

Book title: Linda Harris

Book arranged by Andrew Richardson

Foreword

IT IS no small wonder that when J.R.R. Tolkien came to creating the Shire in his *Lord of the Rings* trilogy, some of his inspiration came from Wiltshire.

This enchanting county no doubt had the same impact on him that it has on the countless others that live and visit here.

And, for the past 150 years, we at the *Wiltshire Times* newspaper have chronicled every heartbeat this amazing county has experienced.

This book captures those memorable events that have made Wiltshire the place it is today, as well as giving you an insight into how our newspaper has played its part in those flashes of history.

From the famous faces that have visited over the years, to major sporting events and Royal engagements, our team was there to seize that moment forever.

And we haven't forgotten to feature some of the mysteries this county is renowned for such as the ancient monument Stonehenge and the first published picture of a crop circle – you'll find it all here.

So we hope you enjoy taking this trip back down memory lane as we look forward to bringing you the next 150 years of news.

Toby Granville
Editor
Wiltshire Times

CHAPTER 1

Wiltshire Times Production and History

The *Wiltshire Times* started life as the *Trowbridge and Wiltshire Advertiser* in May 1854, and was the first newspaper to be published in the county town. At that time it was a monthly penny publication, turning weekly in 1855. Since those early days there have been many changes to the way the popular paper is produced but some things remain the same.

All 10 of the newspaper's editors have stuck steadfastly to the aims of founder Benjamin Lansdown who wanted to give unprecedented prominence to matters of local interest and importance.

Many name changes, altered shapes and the introduction of modern technology over the past 150 years have led to the award-winning weekly tabloid newspaper packed with news, sport and advertising we see today.

Trowbridge Fire Brigade pump shown in front of a *Wiltshire Times* advertising board.

The first edition of the *Trowbridge and Wiltshire Advertiser*, predecessor of the *Wiltshire Times*, published on 6 May 1854.

Printer Benjamin Lansdown, founder of the *Wiltshire Times*, published the first newspaper in Trowbridge in 1854.

The Albion printing press used by Benjamin Lansdown to produce the first year's issues of the *Trowbridge and Wiltshire Advertiser*. He bought the press and a second-hand typewriter from mentor John Sweet for £12.

George Lansdown was the youngest son of Benjamin. He became editor in 1884 on the death of his father and remained in charge for more than 40 years. He died in 1932.

A front page from 1884. The newspaper became the *Wiltshire Times* in 1880.

The *Wiltshire Times* stationery shop and office, Silver Street, Trowbridge. The shop was eventually given up in 1935 when the firm moved all production to the printworks in Duke Street.

Bales of paper are delivered to the *Wiltshire Times* office, Duke Street, Trowbridge, in 1900.

Compositors put together metal type creating words for the newspaper pages. It is believed this picture dates to the early 1900s.

Benjamin Lansdown's eldest son James took on the business side of the newspaper while his brother George was editor.

The newspaper's third editor was James's elder son Charles. He was editor from 1932 to 1940.

George's only son Leonard was already joint managing director of the firm when he took on the editorship after the death of Charles. He was editor from 1940 to 1957.

The Hoe printing press. Rotary presses allowed printers to use continuous rolls of paper instead of individual sheets and considerably sped up the printing process.

Michael Lansdown was the fourth generation of his family to work on the paper and the fifth Lansdown to become editor. He is pictured here with his wife Dorothy.

Michael Lansdown, editor from 1957 to 1981.

An edition of the *Wiltshire Times & News* from 1964.

Copies of the *Wiltshire Times* roll off the printing press in 1965.

Lines (slugs) of type were created by linotype operators using a keyboard – the individual characters formed a line and they were then cast into hot metal. These machines were standard at all newspapers through the 20th century until the 1980s.

Compositors and stone-hands put together blocks of type to create metal pages.

A flexible replica of the metal page was created (stereo), which the foundry workers then used to make printing plates.

A flexible replica of the metal page was created.

Piles of the curved stereo printing plates.

Pages were proofed before the final printing plates were made to check for mistakes, here shown in 1982.

The scene in the composing room, 1982.

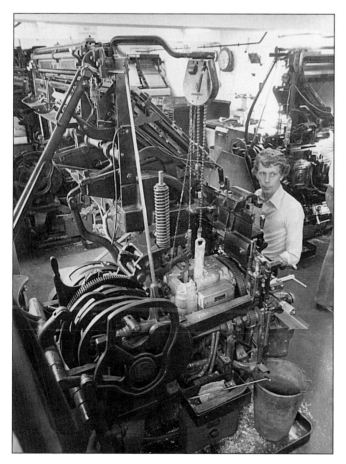

At work on an intertype machine (the same as a linotype machine, but by a different manufacturer).

The linotype room in 1982.

Warren Harding
cleans a plate to
get it ready for
the printing press
in July 1982.

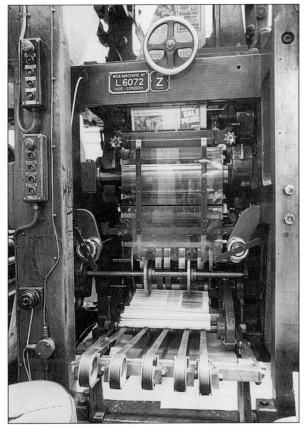

The newspaper being collated in 1982.

The *Wiltshire Times* rolls off the press in 1982.

Four *Wiltshire Times* editors meet at the launch of the new tabloid newspaper in March 2000. From left to right: Jack Brennan (editor 1981 to 1993); Christine Moss (editor 1993 to 1996); Stephen White (editor 1999 to 2001); and Gary Lawrence (editor 1996 to 1998).

Toby Granville, 10th editor of the Wiltshire Times, was appointed at the age of 28. He previously worked in London, starting his career at the age of 17 on the national newspaper *The People*. He is shown here looking at an old printing plate on display at the Trowbridge Museum during the 'Hot Off The Press' exhibition in spring 2004.

The *Wiltshire Times* as it looks in 2004.

Print supervisor Jeff Barrett oversees the printing of the *Wiltshire Times* on the Southampton press where it is now produced. The press is equal to the size of three double-decker buses high and six double-decker buses long.

CHAPTER 2

Wiltshire Times Staff

The *Wiltshire Times* remained in the hands of the Lansdown family for more than a century until it was sold in the early 1960s. Staff were split into a number of departments over the years with editorial, advertising, production, printworks and foundry among them, but as well as hard work there has always been time for fun.

Staff outing to Symonds Yat, 15 June 1907.

The Wiltshire Times staff, 1914.

The *Wiltshire Times* 1st Cricket Eleven from 1921.

A *Wiltshire Times* staff outing to Weymouth on 12 January 1926. The little boy in the front row on the left would be one of the newspaper's future editors, Michael Lansdown.

Wiltshire Times staff outing to Lymington and Yarmouth, 9 June 1928.

Old timers at the *Wiltshire Times*.

Wiltshire Times outing to Weymouth, 1933.

Staff outing to Porthcawl, 20 June 1936.

Wartime dinner party for staff, November 1940.

Wiltshire Times centenary, 1954.

Staff gathered at the retirement of fourth *Wiltshire Times* editor, Leonard Lansdown, on 29 December 1967.

Long-serving *Wiltshire Times* columnist Denis Kingman with wife Jean (left) and County Council chairman Mary Salisbury, marking Denis's 50 years in journalism in 1990.

CHAPTER 3

Famous Faces

Many famous faces from TV and film have visited over the years with *Wiltshire Times* photographers ready to record the occasion. Here are a selection of the stars to be seen in west Wiltshire in recent years.

Anne Aston, co-host of TV's *The Golden Shot*, made a personal appearance at the newly extended Woolworths store in Chippenham on 18 April 1975.

Radio 4's Brian Johnston interviews silversmith apprentice Chris Stevens in Lacock for the *Down Your Way* programme, 25 July 1975.

Dr Who TV star Tom Baker visited Martin's newsagents in Trowbridge for a Target Books promotion and autograph session in July 1975.

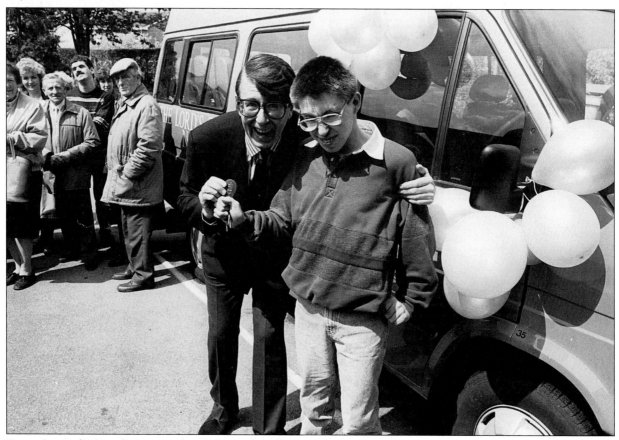

Entertainer Leslie Crowther presented a minibus to the Ashton Street Centre, Trowbridge, in May 1991.

Sitcom stars Terry Scott and June Whitfield helped with a store promotion at Waldens Supermarket, Trowbridge, in 1986.

Star of the silver screen Margaret Lockwood attended the opening of the Gaumont Cinema, Trowbridge, in 1937. The cinema seated 1,200 people and opened with a showing of *King Solomon's Mines*.

A petition against the introduction of a cinema entertainment tax in May 1951.

Comedians Arthur Askey and Dickie Henderson provided entertainment at the opening of Corsham's pedestrianised high street in March 1976.

The filming of Moll Flanders in Lacock.

Politician Tony Benn addressing a rally of NUPE workers in Trowbridge, 28 February 1981.

Wiltshire tourist attraction Longleat celebrated its crystal anniversary in April 1981. The then Lord Bath can be seen cutting the cake with one of the Chipperfield chimps.

Lacock has been a popular film location for many years. Here crews can be seen at work filming *Kipps* in October 1940.

CHAPTER 4

Sport

Sport has always been a key factor in the popularity of local newspapers with results and match reports a popular source of information. Over the years many sporting heroes have graced the pages of the *Wiltshire Times* alongside our own local sports stars.

Australian international cricketer Geoff Marsh in action in Trowbridge.

Race days at Castle Combe often provide dramatic moments to capture on camera. Here is one of many spectacular crash scenes caught on film by *Wiltshire Times* photographers.

Olympic sprinting star
Linford Christie signs
autographs for fans.

The Kellogg's Cycle Tour of Britain passes through Staverton in 1990. The Old Bear pub can be seen in the background.

Legendary race horse Red Rum was guest of honour at the opening of a new restaurant at the Farmhouse Inn, Southwick, in 1990.

Wrestling star Giant Haystacks is here seen in action at the Civic Hall, Trowbridge, in February 1989.

Farleigh motorcycle scramble, June 1938.

Trowbridge Town FC, Western League Champions, May 1940.

The two openers for Trowbridge cricket team leaving the pavilion, May 1950.

Trowbridge cricket team leaving the reconstructed pavilion, May 1950.

Chippenham Town FC team, 1949.

Golfer Ian Woosnam opens Thoulstone Park Golf Club, near Chapmanslade, in October 1992.

Olympic swimmer Sharron Davies joined pupils for the annual Clarendon School fun run in Trowbridge, April 1992.

Olympic sprinter Linford Christie had attended the Clarendon School fun run in March 1991.

CHAPTER 5

Royal Visits and Events

Youngsters enjoying a drink from their Coronation mugs in Melksham, May 1937.

The proclamation of George VI, Trowbridge Town Hall.

HRH Princess Anne inspecting the ratings at HMS *Royal Arthur* naval training base near Corsham, 1986. The base is now closed and is home to a business park.

The Queen at RAF Lyneham, home of Hercules aircraft, 1990.

Queen Mary visits Holt in May 1940.

Queen Mary is greeted by workers at the Haden's factory, Trowbridge.

A party to celebrate the royal wedding of Prince Charles and Lady Diana Spencer at The Homestead, Trowbridge, in July 1981.

The royal wedding party in Rock Road, Trowbridge.

Residents in Hardens Mead, Chippenham, held a fancy
dress party to celebrate the royal wedding in 1981.

Residents of Downing Street, Chippenham, preparing for the Queen's
Silver Jubilee street party in 1977.

Corsham Jubilee thanksgiving service, June 1977.

Crowds await the arrival of Prince Charles at Bradford on Avon, June 2003.

Prince Charles visits the West Barn, Bradford on Avon, June 2003.

The Princess Royal is a regular visitor to the Dorothy House Hospice in Winsley. Here she receives a posy of flowers from Amy Schofield, whose mother was cared for at the hospice, September 2003.

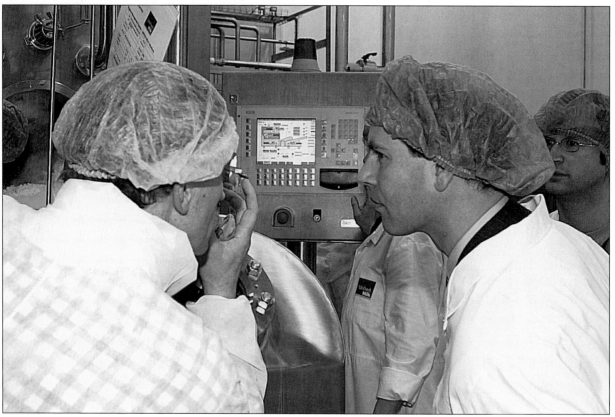

Prince Edward views a process at the former United Milk dairy, Westbury. January 2003.

Sophie, Countess of Wessex, meets pre-school youngsters at the new Westbury Leigh School, July 2004.

Sophie chats to pupils at Westbury Leigh School.

The royal couple, Edward and Sophie, were amused to hear children's ideas about how the royals spend their day. July 2004.

The Queen visited Chippenham in December 2001.

The Duke of Edinburgh in Chippenham.

The Queen in Chippenham.

Prince Charles meets soldiers of the Black Watch in Warminster before they go out to Iraq, August 2004.

CHAPTER 6

Wartime and Military Connections

West Wiltshire is an area ripe with military history. The wartime effort was immense with ammunition and Spitfire factories as well as military bases spread across the region. Everyone played their part. Today the *Wiltshire Times'* patch includes the garrison town of Warminster on the edge of Salisbury Plain.

Wiltshire VADs demonstrate how to use gas masks.

Chippenham Remembrance parade, 20 November 1937.

Peace protesters in 1986 at RAF Rudloe Manor, Westwells Road, Corsham, said to be the home of a 'nuclear bunker' and secret military communications base.

A World War One reader of
the *Wiltshire Times*.

Trowbridge was home to a Spitfire aircraft factory during the war when one of the town's engineering firms took over production. Seen here are employees from the factory in Bradley Road.

The factory floor.

A Spitfire taking off.

Long since disused, the Spitfire factory works are demolished.

Ammunitions workers during World War Two pose
for a staff photograph with the range of products they
produce.

More recent times. Soldiers showing off the SA80 rifle
at a Firepower demonstration on the ranges at
Warminster.

Hercules aircraft celebrate clocking up one million air miles in 1990.

Police find an ammo dump at a farmhouse in Rowde.

Army training at a new 'Fighting In Built Up Areas' village created at Copehill Down on Salisbury Plain, 1990.

Melksham, April 1940. St Michael's Dig for Victory.

Two pictures of Trowbridge ARP exercises at The Conigre, January 1940.

Proclamation at Trowbridge Town Hall, 1930s.

An old tank being broken up for scrap in Trowbridge Park, July 1940.

Old boilers at Studley Mills were used as air raid shelters. April 1939.

Chippenham War Weapons Week parade, May 1941.

Digging for Victory, County Hall, Trowbridge, May 1942.

Land Army Girls.

The last display of historic aircraft at RAF Colerne's museum goes on show before the collection was sold. August 1975.

CHAPTER 7
Showtime and Events

Corsham May Queen Procession, 21 May 1938.

Entertainer Fred Wedlock at the West Wilts Show.

Circus characters in Fore Street,
Trowbridge, May 1936.

Bradford on Avon waif and stray pageant, April 1938.

Bradford on Avon's Coronation clock is refurbished for the Queen's Golden Jubilee.

Balloon festival: scenery from the skies.

Longleat balloon festival.

Corsham Dickens festival in progress in the High Sltreet, December 1985.

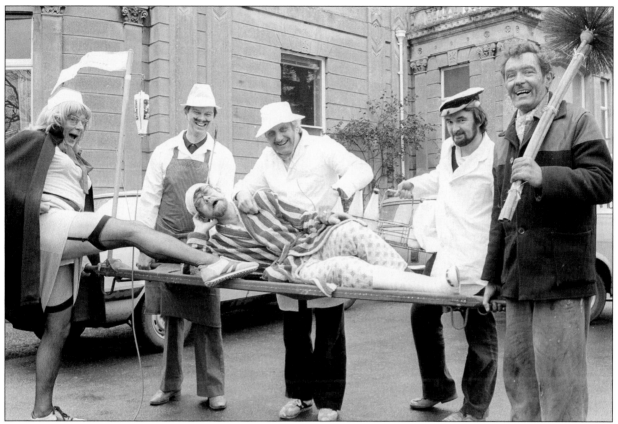

Bradford on Avon hospital stretcher race, May 1981.

Holt lawnmower races, 1981.

The tug of war contest at Lackham Young Farmers' show, May 1981.

Music Festival, 1925.

Winsley playgroup celebrates its 21st anniversary, June 1988.

Trowbridge Carnival baby show winners, 1990.

Crowds at Chippenham Folk Festival, 1990.

The presentation of a radio set in the 1930s.

Trowbridge Christmas lights switch on, 1990.

Avon Rubber employees celebrate a wedding at Great Chalfield Manor, 1938.

Chippenham cage birds show, 1952.

Dairy students day at Spye Park, 1951.

Westbury Labour Club's children's party, January 1951.

Lacock Abbey fete with Miss Talbot, July 1951.

Unigate Gala day competitors ready for 'It's A Knockout' games, 20 June 1975.

The Wee Willie Winkie float from Dilton Marsh carnival procession, 30 May 1975.

The 'Gangster' float from Trowbridge carnival, 19 September 1975.

Lacock and Chippenham Folk Festival. A parade of morris men in Lacock High Street, 30 May 1975.

CHAPTER 8
Major Incidents

Wiltshire Times photographers have attended the scene of thousands of incidents of concern to readers. Here are a selection of the dramatic pictures taken over the years.

Fire at Chapman's factory, Trowbridge, 1951.

A major blaze on a trailer carrying straw damaged a house in Mount Pleasant, Bradford on Avon, in August 1993.

Hilperton Village Hall was destroyed by fire in July 1939. Residents are shown viewing the remains.

The Chippenham Bomb

A 1,000lb World War Two bomb was discovered after investigations at the site of a proposed third secondary school for Chippenham in February 1997. More than 1,000 people were evacuated from their homes while Army bomb disposal experts were called in to deal with it. Fat Boy and a smaller 500lb bomb were detonated by Army bomb disposal officer Capt Peter Shields after his attempts to defuse them failed.

The hole army bomb disposal officers were working down.

Detonation!

At work with one of the bombs.

Captain Peter Shields.

Proceeding with care.

One of the World War Two bombs discovered at the proposed school site near Hardens Mead.

A stand at Trowbridge Town Football Club burns down in the early 1980s.

Inferno. Firefighters checking out the scene, Green Lane, Trowbridge, in 1995.

Three pictures of St James's Church, Trowbridge, damaged by the storm of 1990.

Six pictures show a fire at the Avon factory, Melksham, in 1966 which caused £1 million of damage. Eighty homes next to the site were evacuated.

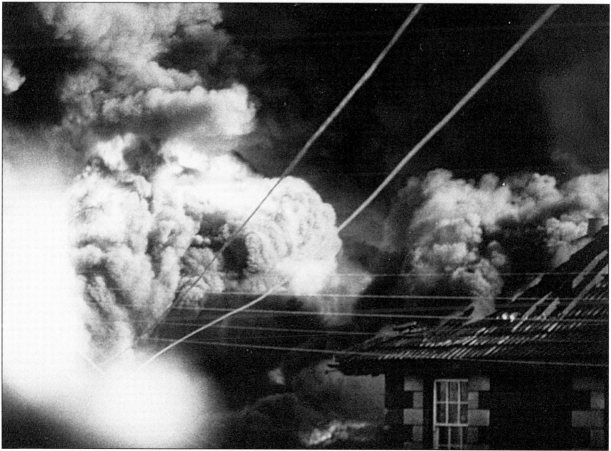

Pages from the *Wiltshire Times* reporting the event.

Fire at the Elephant and Castle pub, Castle Street, Trowbridge, in 1992. The pub was severely damaged and later demolished.

Fire destroyed the roof of the Park Lane Motor Hotel, Corsham, in 1990. The motel never reopened for business.

Fire at Home Mills, Trowbridge, 1930s.

CHAPTER 9
National Events

Hostage Terry Waite returns to Britain, 1991.

John McCarthy flew back to RAF Lyneham being released from captivity after being held hostage in the Lebanon. He met UN secretary general Perez de Cuellar and foreign minister Douglas Hogg at Lyneham following his return in 1991.

Hundreds of journalists from around the world, including the *Wiltshire Times*, were at RAF Lyneham for the return of John McCarthy in 1991.

Protesters against the Poll Tax try to enter a meeting at West Wiltshire District Council, 1990.

Good humoured but boisterous football fans prompted a police response at the height of World Cup fever in 2002.

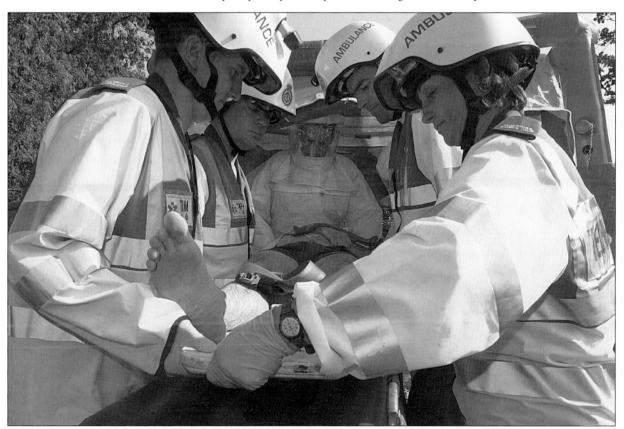

Wiltshire Ambulance Service show off some of the new decontamination equipment made compulsory by the Government after fears about how the country would respond to terrorist attacks.

Foot and Mouth precautions at Countrywide Farmers, Melksham.

A suspected outbreak of foot and mouth disease at a Wiltshire farm led to burning of carcasses.

The Foot and Mouth warning sign became a regular sight around Wiltshire.

Fire strike pickets, November 2002.

Firefighters walk out at Trowbridge fire station during national fire strikes, January 2003.

The fuel crisis, September 2001.

Queues at Atworth at the height of the nationwide fuel crisis.

CHAPTER 10
Off the Wall

The 'Tamworth Two' pigs escaped on their way to the abattoir gaining notoriety in the national and local press, as well as being the subject of a TV film.

The Staverton factory clock is removed for scrap, 1935.

School milk in 1935.

A Trowbridge bus conductor with his 2s 6d reward after finding £2,000 in 1935.

A sealion escapes from
Longleat, near Warminster,
and is found in
Trowbridge Park duck
pond, July 1988.

Frenchman Jacques Aubree sets up an 'edible snail' farm at Rode near Trowbridge, August 1988.

Giant lemons being weighed for a world record bid at
Lackham College of Agriculture, November 1988.

Brewery boss TC Usher with a yard of ale, Trowbridge, 1930s.

Chippenham Amateur Tobacco Growers' exhibition, March 1951.

Jonathan Clark with his adopted pet rook at St Augustine's RC School, Trowbridge, 1990.

CHAPTER 11
In All Weathers

Children at Lacock School making the most of a snowfall in 1986.

Milkman in the flood at Staverton, 1935.

Floods are a familiar sight at Staverton each year.

'Witches' house at Bradford on Avon.

Stourhead in snow, 1996.

CHAPTER 12
Buildings

Stately home Rood Ashton House, near Trowbridge, the home of the Long family, faces demolition in May 1975.

The rededication of Winsley church bells, June 1951.

The new swimming pool in Trowbridge, 1939.

Trowbridge pool, 1981.

The Emery Gate shopping centre under construction in Chippenham, 1988.

Work starts on building The Shires shopping centre, Trowbridge. The view from Bythesea Road, 1988.

Melksham High Street before traffic lights were installed at the junction with Church Street, 1986.

Westinghouse workers leaving the Chippenham factory at the end of shift, 1986.

Rooftop view of the new Emery Gate shopping centre being built in Chippenham, 1986. The old North Wiltshire District Council offices are just visible through the trees in the background.

Opening of the new Kinema, Trowbridge, 1934.

Melksham Hospital opens, 30 July 1938.

Opening of the new Seymour Estate, Trowbridge, 20 July 1935.

Inside the George Hotel, Trowbridge, a former town centre landmark but derelict in 1981.

CHAPTER 13
Wiltshire at Work and Play

The 1st Devizes Cubs are here seen taking part in a world record attempt to visit all seven of Wiltshire's white horses in a day. This group are at the Westbury White Horse, 20 June 1975.

Horse-racing pundit John McCririk opens a new betting shop in Castle Street, Trowbridge, in April 1992.

Devizes dustmen go on strike over the sacking of a colleague, August 1975.

Corsham Town Band, 1930s.

Calne handbell ringers, June 1938.

Trowbridge character Ron Brewer outside the *Wiltshire Times* office.

Lord Bath at the opening of his mirror maze at Longleat, April 1998.

Veteran anti-poll tax campaigner Archie MacGregor of Trowbridge, 1990.

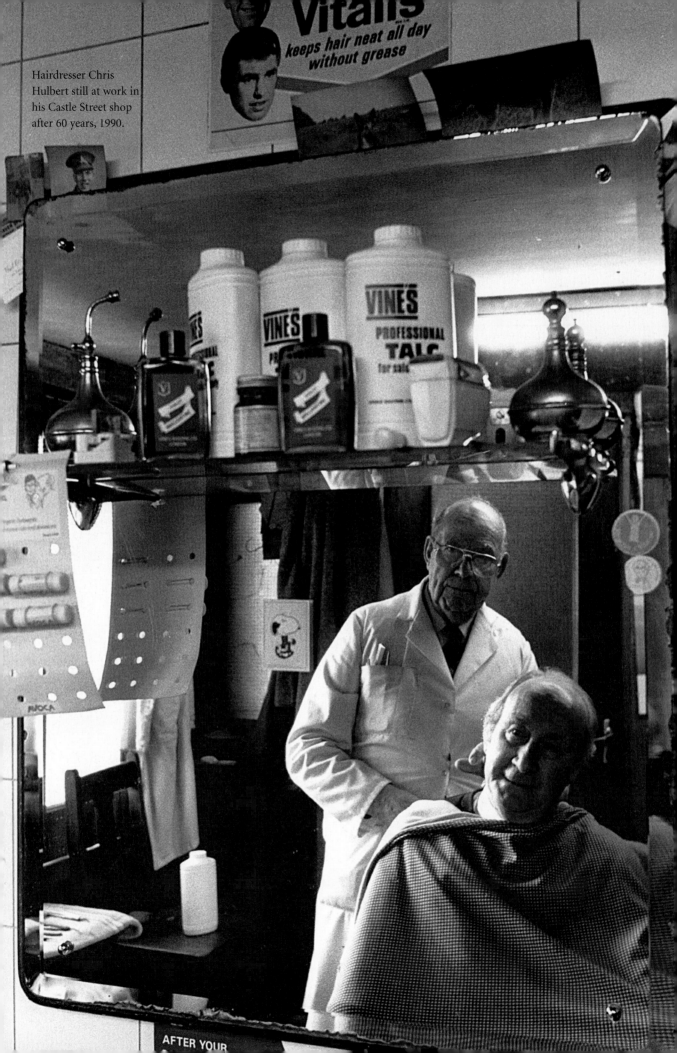

Hairdresser Chris Hulbert still at work in his Castle Street shop after 60 years, 1990.

A new fire tender at Trowbridge fire station, March 1951.

Women porters at Trowbridge railway station, March 1941.

A presentation at Bradford on Avon railway station, 1952.

A biplane crashes at Semington, 2 April 1938.

A GWR railcar at Trowbridge railway station, 22 February 1936.

A bridge is removed in Trowbridge.

Children leaving Trowbridge station by train for the seaside, June 1938.

The Royal Bath and West Show, 1990.

Melksham
Agricultural Show,
November 1938.

Farming with a vintage plough.

CHAPTER 14
School Days

George Ward School chess club team, Melksham, 1976.

Comic Relief day at Matravers School, Westbury, March 1991. Pupil Che Rodwell endures maggots down his trousers for charity. Samantha Kent does the honours.

A view of the old Chippenham Technical School.

Walwayne Court Primary opens in Trowbridge, September 1991. Headteacher Richard Brown and some pupils.

Trowbridge Adcroft Girls School – standard IV – 1927.

Newtown and Trinity School, Trowbridge, sponsored fun run, 1990.

Winners of Westbury Leigh Junior School's music
festival, April 1990.

BBC weather presenter Tony
Targett visiting Paxcroft
School, Trowbridge, April
1990.

Lowbourne Infants School, Melksham, presented with a new computer by fundraisers, 1990.

Rain stopped play for pupils at Keevil School, May 1991.

Fun in the snow at Edington Primary School, February 1991.

Codford School fancy dress day for Book Week, 1991.

Lacock School donkey derby at the May fair, May 1990.

Circus clown Philipo entertains pupils at Holbrook School, Trowbridge, May 2002.

Quiet reflection for pupils at Holt School as they watch the Queen Mother's funeral, April 2002.

Sutton Veny School holds its annual ANZAC memorial service, April 2003.

Wingfield School's 150th anniversary celebrations, May 2002.

Steeple Ashton School announces its closure after more than 100 years, October 2003.

Dotty Day at Winsley School. Pupils Isobel Sheppard and Robyn Hepple help launch Dorothy House hospice's charity fundraising day.

Pupils at Staverton School re-enact Coronation Day to celebrate the Queen's Golden Jubilee, May 2002.

North Bradley School pupils practise their handwriting skills, June 2003.

Neston School links up with the International Space Station, July 2003.

CHAPTER 15
Mysterious Wiltshire

Whether it is crop circles, white horses or stone formations, the beautiful countryside of Wiltshire has its fair share of magic and mystery.

Stonehenge is one of Wiltshire's best-loved tourist attractions and its spiritual heritage draws thousands of visitors each year. The Summer Solstice brings with it thousands of druids, New Age travellers and people wishing to view sunrise on the longest day of the year. In the 1980s there were regular clashes between travellers, who were trying to gain access to the stones, and police, but in recent years Stonehenge has been opened up to allow public access for peaceful worship and festivities to take place.

In 1980 the *Wiltshire Times* became the first newspaper ever to publish a photograph of a crop circle and since then they have become a regular feature in the fields of Wiltshire and around the world.

For more information about Wiltshire's mysterious phenomena visit our website: www.weirdwiltshire.co.uk

Stonehenge

Winter Solstice at Stonehenge, December 1989.

The Thin Blue Line. Photographer Trevor Porter captured the scene as thousands of people swarmed over the brow of a hill on their way to Stonehenge. Just a few police officers can be seen blocking their path at the height of the Stonehenge troubles in 1986.

Drummers taking part in a torch-lit procession in front of 24,000 revellers at the stones in 2002.

Rolo Maughling, Archdruid of Glastonbury, with Denny Price and Wendy de Vine, with the flowers of summer prior to conducting a ceremony at the stones.

A police presence at Stonehenge summer solstice festivities.

The scene at Stonehenge as thousands attend the ancient monument to celebrate.

Nearly 30,000 people attended the summer solstice at Stonehenge in June 2003.

Connie as the Glastonbury Fairy at Stonehenge for the solstice.

The 2003 event is said to have been the best summer solstice in living memory, with the most spectacular sunrise for years.

The summer solstice in 2003 was the fourth year English Heritage allowed open access to the stones so people could celebrate the dawn of the longest day of the year.

Crop Circles

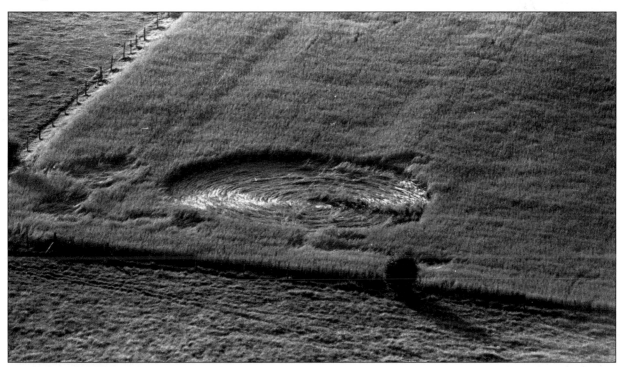

The first published photograph of a crop circle appeared in the *Wiltshire Times*. Three mysterious circles appeared in a field of oats below the gaze of the White Horse, Westbury, in 1980.

A corn circle appeared in a field near Bratton, off the Westbury to Bratton Road, in July 1994.

Crop circles in a field near Cley Hill, Warminster, July 1995.

The first of the year's crop circles appears in a field between Westbury and Bratton, June 1995.

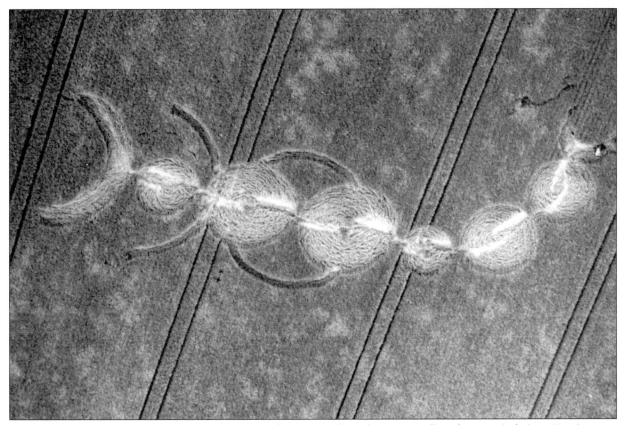

Over the years crop circles developed from what were at first just simple circles into complicated geometric designs. Here is a view of one in a Wiltshire field taken from the air.

CHAPTER 16
Then and Now

A popular feature in the *Wiltshire Times* in recent years has been the nostalgic Then and Now section. Each week we chronicle a picture from days gone by and then recreate the street scene in modern times. Here are a selection of such images from our files.

Market Street, Bradford on Avon, 2003.

Fore Street, Trowbridge, looking towards Wicker Hill, 1948.

Fore Street to Wicker Hill, Trowbridge, 2002.

Market Street, Bradford on Avon, 1903.

Trowbridge Fire Brigade, 1910.

Trowbridge Fire Brigade, 2003.

Church Walk, Trowbridge, 1905.

Church Walk, Trowbridge, 2003.

Warminster High Street, 1907.

Warminster High Street, 2002.

Edward Street, Westbury, 1920s.

Edward Street, Westbury, 2002.

Market Place, Melksham, 1907.

Market Place, Melksham, 2002.

Ushers garage, Trowbridge, in the 1930s.

Parade in Newtown, Trowbridge, 1907.

Floods in Market Street, Bradford on Avon.

Zion Baptist Church, Trowbridge, 1913.

Trowbridge Red Cross hospital.

Bradford Road, Trowbridge in 1913.

Market Street, Bradford on Avon, 1903.